Original title:
Brambles and Banter

Copyright © 2025 Creative Arts Management OÜ
All rights reserved.

Author: Henry Beaumont
ISBN HARDBACK: 978-1-80567-440-5
ISBN PAPERBACK: 978-1-80567-739-0

The Lively Tangle

In the garden where giggles roam,
Twists and turns, a playful home.
Socks on hands, oh what a sight,
Chasing shadows till the night.

A cat with a crown, oh what a queen,
Dancing amid the leaves so green.
Laughter bounces off each wall,
In this maze, we trip and fall.

Bright Blooms and Cheeky Grins

Flower hats on silly heads,
Tickling toes in flower beds.
A breeze that whispers silly tales,
As laughter rides on fluttering sails.

Bouncing bumbles take a spin,
Wobble, jiggle, big silly grin.
With each turn, the petals sway,
In joyous chaos, we will play.

Comedy in the Greenery

Leaves are laughing, don't you hear?
Twirling critters, full of cheer.
With a hop and a funny dance,
Nature joins the wild romance.

In the bushes, giggles hide,
A squirrel pauses, eyes open wide.
Muffled chuckles fill the air,
Who knew nature had such flair?

Mirth among the Mumble

Whispers rustle, secrets tease,
Bouncing off the playful breeze.
A tiny frog with quite the leap,
Jumps into a pile, making a heap.

Giggles run among the vines,
Where sunlight dances, and joy shines.
In every twist, a smile's found,
In the chatter, we're forever bound.

Chortles in the Brush

A ticklish vine crept near my shoe,
It whispered jokes that only grew.
I stumbled, laughed, and took a fall,
As thorns erupted, a noisy brawl.

With every step, a giggle burst,
Nature's humor, almost cursed.
A dandy thicket, clever and sly,
Inviting chuckles as I passed by.

Drollery in the Grove

In the grove where shadows dance,
The squirrels plotted their next prance.
They tossed acorns like wry puns,
While I clapped hands and chewed on buns.

A tree trunk whispered tales of glee,
With each bark, a new decree.
Laughter echoed, a merry fight,
As leaves joined in, a fluttering sight.

Mirth Among the Ivy

Twisted tendrils hid a grin,
With every rustle, a new joke spun.
The ivy chuckled, shook with glee,
As I tried to climb its leafy spree.

The garden's path turned into fun,
Where flowers danced, and won the run.
Each petal playfully took a poke,
In a world where laughter never broke.

Snarls of Celebration

In tangled knots, the laughter grew,
A party started, wild and new.
Beneath the branches, antics bloomed,
As I slipped on roots and nearly fumed.

The cheerful shrubs, in secret glee,
Held a festival just for me.
Snickers floated on the breeze,
Making merriment with perfect ease.

Entangled in Jests

A tangle of words, a twist of delight,
Where laughter erupts, the day feels just right.
With quips in the air, we dance 'round the sun,
In a forest of chuckles, we're never outdone.

We trip on our feet, with giggles we sway,
In the thicket of fun, we've all come to play.
With pokes and with prods, the jests start to bloom,
In the shade of the trees, we banish our gloom.

Sharp Leaves and Light Hearts

The leaves rustle softly, a tickle of glee,
With each sharp remark, we're as light as can be.
In the shade of the greens, we find our true pace,
With laughter as bright as the sun on our face.

We weave through the bushes, our wit in full swing,
Each jest a small bird, on a bright, flapping wing.
With every small poke, our spirits ignite,
In the garden of jests, everything feels right.

The Playful Snare

Caught in a trap of our own clever wit,
Each punchline a twig, each laughter a hit.
Entwined in the joy, we spring up and down,
With every retort, we're the jesters of town.

The snare of our humor, it's tangled and skilled,
In the forest of jokes, our hearts are fulfilled.
With a tap on the shoulder, we gleefully thrive,
In the web of our banter, we feel so alive!

Twisted Roots of Laughter

Down in the soil, where the quirks tend to grow,
The roots of our humor twist down below.
With each hearty laugh, we nourish the ground,
In the thicket of fun, we're joyfully bound.

Our lives are a jest, and the punchlines are bold,
In the warmth of a smile, new stories unfold.
With playful exchanges, our spirits will soar,
In the dance of the light, we'll forever explore.

Laughter's Labyrinth

In the thicket, laughter hides,
Giggles dance where mischief bides.
A squirrel's prank, a bee's own song,
In this maze, we all belong.

Twisted paths and tangled jokes,
The trees whisper, tease like folks.
A rabbit leaps, a hedgehog grins,
In this nonsense, joy begins.

Leaves are tickled, nightingale sings,
Jests abound on sunny swings.
Sticks entangle, but fear not,
For every slip, there's laughter caught.

With every turn, new jest is found,
In this snarl, we laugh unbound.
So let us wander, come what may,
In our folly, we'll laugh and play.

Folly of the Forest Floor

Among the roots, a badger sprawls,
While cheeky foxes share their brawls.
A turtle trips, a snail gives chase,
In this folly, we find our place.

Mushrooms chuckle, daisies beam,
As we plot and scheme our dream.
The sun dips low, the shadows play,
In this mischief, we'll find our way.

A turtle's waddle, a toad's loud croak,
They rib and nudge, it's all a joke.
Each mishap a story, each laugh a cheer,
In the forest's heart, there's nothing to fear.

So join the dance, let laughter fly,
Swirl with the leaves, under the sky.
In this place where folly thrives,
We find the joy that truly drives.

Thorns and Whimsy

In the garden where we play,
A tickle from a thorny stray.
Laughter spills like morning dew,
As we dodge that prickly view.

Chasing shadows, what a spree,
With crooks and bends, let it be free.
A giggle here, a poke or two,
Oh, how the antics seem to brew.

Follies dance on leafy trails,
While the sun sets with funny tales.
We trip and tumble, but who cares?
Just take a leap, it's full of flares!

So take my hand, let's twine and twist,
In this playful thicket, you can't resist.
With each little jab, we just can't stop,
For laughter blooms at every hop.

A Tangle of Words

In a jumbled mess we meet,
Words collide like dancing feet.
Mirth erupts like sudden sprout,
With every slip, there's laughter out.

Awkward phrases take a spin,
Who knew tongue-tied was a win?
Chortles rise on gusty winds,
As we weave the tales like twins.

Mismatched lines and playful gleam,
Create a picture, or is it a dream?
Rhymes get tangled in our glee,
As every word whispers, "Let's be free!"

So join this frolic, chaos thrives,
With chubby giggles, our fun derives.
Each twist of phrase, a silly jest,
In this tangle, we feel the best.

The Thorny Path of Laughter

On a path that's full of strife,
Joints and jabs create the life.
Step with care, avoid the snare,
For humor lies in what we share.

Poking fun at every turn,
Through the bristles, laughter burns.
We hop along with grins so wide,
As silliness is our trusty guide.

Witty jabs as we stroll by,
With each poke, there's a sigh.
We navigate the snags in play,
For joy is found in every sway.

So come, dear friend, let's romp along,
In this thorny nook where we belong.
With laughter loud and spirits bright,
We'll dance through shadows, chasing light.

Whispers Among the Vines

In the hush where shadows creep,
Whispered giggles, secrets leap.
Amid the twists, a merry fight,
With winks and nods, we ignite the night.

Veils of vines hide silly dreams,
Laughter flows in bubbling streams.
With each rustle, a chuckle grows,
A game of whispers, anything goes!

Through the leaves, our jokes entwine,
In the dark, our joy will shine.
So listen close, don't miss the cue,
For giddy tales are waiting for you.

In this cozy nook, let spirits soar,
With every laugh, you'll want more.
So pluck a dream from tangled reeds,
And let the humor plant its seeds.

Snagged Smiles

In the garden, laughter flies,
A playful dance beneath the skies.
With tangled threads we weave our jest,
Each stumble leads to smiles, the best.

Petals drift like silly tales,
While giggles ride on breezy gales.
A poke, a prod, a gentle tease,
Nature's whims put hearts at ease.

Beneath the thorny, twisted maze,
We chase the sun and bask in praise.
For every slip and silly fall,
We'll hold our joy, we'll have a ball.

So gather 'round and share a cheer,
For in these thickets, laughter's near.
With every grin, we'll find our way,
Through wily paths where children play.

Frolics by the Briers

In hide-and-seek among the thorns,
We trip in laughter, hearts adorn.
A tumble here, a giggle there,
Each twist unveils a new affair.

Wit sprouts like weeds in sunny spaces,
Our jests turn sly in playful races.
With every step, a mischief springs,
We dance like jesters, with silly flings.

The shadows play on our carefree game,
As wildflowers chuckle at our fame.
We weave through blooms while teasing fate,
In tangled moments, we elate.

So take a leap, make a quip,
Through leafy trails, we'll laugh and slip.
With friends beside, the world is bright,
In frolics where we spark delight.

Puns in the Hedge

Amidst the leaves, the laughter grows,
A clever quip that slyly flows.
We pun and play in leafy beds,
With jests that dance upon our heads.

A thorny comment, sharp and bold,
The kind of humor that never gets old.
With giggles poking through the glade,
We find our joy, our grand charade.

The sun sets low, a golden hue,
As puns arise like morning dew.
With every pun, we raise a cheer,
In hedge-bound laughter, we persevere.

So join the fun, don't feel outdone,
For wit creates a world of fun.
Through tangled wit, our spirits soar,
In laughter's grasp, we want for more.

Vines of Vagary

In winding paths where whimsy plays,
We lose our way in quirky ways.
The vines entangle thoughts and schemes,
In playful twists of silly dreams.

A hop, a skip, we dare to glide,
Through jests and giggles, side by side.
With every snag, a chuckle blooms,
Through nature's jest, our joy consumes.

So let us twirl in tangled fray,
With cheeky grins, we'll find our way.
For in the forest's gentle fold,
Each twist anew, a story told.

Embrace the ride, embrace the spree,
In murmurings of mystery.
With laughter's vines to guide our roam,
In whimsy's watch, we'll find our home.

Sprouts of Laughter

In the garden where giggles grow,
A rabbit tripped on a toe.
The flowers danced with great delight,
As butterflies giggled, taking flight.

The sunbeams tickled the grassy floor,
While a puppy rolled, wanting more.
A parrot squawked a witty joke,
And everyone laughed 'til they nearly choked.

The ladybug wore a tiny grin,
Sipping dew from a cup of gin.
Beneath the stems, a party brewed,
With snickers and chuckles, quite the mood!

With pumpkins laughing, big and round,
And squirrels bounding, joyous sound.
In this patch, joy is the seed,
Sprouting smiles from root to bead.

Revelry in the Ramble

Through tangled vines, we'll skip and sway,
A hedgehog's antics brightening the day.
The frogs croak tunes that tickle the air,
As giggles pop up like grass everywhere.

Beneath the willow, antics abound,
A jester raccoon, prancing around.
Chasing shadows and imitating a dance,
Each silly move a chance for a chance.

The ants throw a party, snacks and more,
While crickets play tunes that everyone adores.
Laughter spills over, as friends all unite,
In a whirl of mirth under soft moonlight.

With playful whispers and jests so grand,
Where nature's laughter is close at hand.
Let's frolic in silliness, come take a ride,
In the woods where whimsy and joy collide.

Banter Beneath the Boughs

Two squirrels chattered in the high treetops,
Exchanging tales of their latest flops.
One fell asleep and tumbled to ground,
While the other just chuckled, spinning around.

A snail took a stroll, slow and serene,
While daisies whispered, "Oh, what a scene!"
They shared sweet jokes about the sun's warm rays,
And giggled at shadows casting silly plays.

The wise old owl hooted a tune,
Dropping puns while the crickets croon.
With every flutter of leaves overhead,
Came bursts of laughter from bright flower beds.

Together they bask in nature's glow,
Turning tiny mishaps into the best show.
Under the branches, humor takes flight,
Beneath boughs that cradle pure delight.

Laughter with the Leaves

In the midst of fall, leaves start to twirl,
A floppy fox spins in a whirl.
With crinkly sounds, they rustle and tease,
While pumpkins giggle, feeling at ease.

A family of owls in a game of disguise,
With glasses and hats, they all look wise.
While mischief brews in acorn tree trunks,
A chipmunk winks, and the laughter debunks.

Mice play tag with the soft autumn breeze,
Whisking by flowers, just as they please.
Each hitch of a paw sets off more cheer,
With chatter so bright for all to hear.

As the sun dips low, painting skies bright,
The woodland friends gather, a delightful sight.
With every chuckle beneath colored trees,
Laughter from leaves carries on the breeze.

Sprigs of Sarcasm

In the garden where mischief grows,
A smile hides where trouble sows.
With snickers and snorts, we weave a tale,
As laughter blooms and worries pale.

The petals giggle in the breeze,
While the trees nod with amusing ease.
Frogs croak jokes as they leap,
In this riot where secrets seep.

Petty squabbles, oh what a sight,
Fluffy clouds mock the day and night.
Chasing shadows, we trip and dance,
In a world where fools take a chance.

So join the fray, let sarcasm reign,
With every quip, forget the pain.
In this playground where quirkiness sings,
We toast to the joy that laughter brings.

Tangles of Jest

Underneath the tangled vines,
Witty thoughts spring up like pines.
With giggles and grins, we share the floor,
In a circus where none can ignore.

The bees buzz tales of silly plight,
A caterpillar in a wild costume invites.
While the sun winks at our clever jive,
We navigate humor to feel alive.

Every poke and playful tease,
Brings forth laughter with such ease.
In the midst of jests, friendships thrive,
Like crazy ants on a sugar dive.

So let's embrace this knotty fun,
With every quirk, a spark begun.
In tangled delight, we spend our time,
Crafting memories, oh so sublime.

Laughter Beneath the Boughs

Beneath the boughs where shadows play,
Laughter rises, come what may.
Tickles of jest in a light-hearted breeze,
Whispers and giggles, just aim to please.

A squirrel narrates his mighty quest,
While birds chirp back, they never rest.
In this wild theater, antics unfold,
With tales of daring, both brave and bold.

The sun peeks through with a cheeky grin,
As we play hide and seek, our fun to begin.
Each sly remark a feathered dart,
In this joyous game that fills the heart.

Embrace the echoes of cheerful cheer,
For in each laugh, there's love held dear.
Under branches where we freely roam,
In laughter's embrace, we feel at home.

Quips in the Underbrush

Amidst the thickets, quips do sprout,
With snide remarks and playful shout.
Witty banter weaves through the air,
As laughter dances without a care.

The rabbits gossip, the hedgehogs snicker,
Every wisecrack makes the moments quicker.
In shady nooks where secrets lie,
We share our tales, let worries fly.

With twigs for microphones, they share their quirks,
Outlandish stories made of smirks.
Dewdrops shimmer like teasing eyes,
In this folly, fun never dies.

So wander here where silliness blooms,
In the underbrush, dispelling glooms.
Quips galore under nature's hush,
Engaging laughter in a lovely rush.

Whimsy in the Woods

In the forest where squirrels scheme,
A raccoon plots like it's a dream.
The trees giggle at the show,
While shadows dance in the afterglow.

A rabbit tries to sing a tune,
But ends up croaking like a loon.
The mushrooms sway with such delight,
As crickets join in the starry night.

A fox with flair takes center stage,
While leaves flip pages, turning the page.
A dance-off breaks 'tween beetles and ants,
In nature's arena, everyone pranced.

So if you wander through this glee,
Beware the jokes from the old oak tree.
With laughter thick as dawn's fresh dew,
Your heart will bloom, just like a flower too.

The Joyful Clutch of Nature

The wind whispers secrets to the moss,
While owls play games without a toss.
With every branch that starts to sway,
Nature chuckles in a vibrant way.

Squirrels in hats leap and bound,
Their mischievous giggles echo around.
A bear in shades struts with pride,
While a raccoon chef stirs up a tide.

The sun throws rays like confetti bright,
As flowers sway, the colors ignite.
Each petal a laugh, each stem a cheer,
In this wood of joy, there's nothing to fear.

So take a stroll and join the spree,
Let nature's jokes set your heart free.
Embrace the mirth, the wild dance,
In this joyful clutch, take a chance.

Thorns of Whimsy

Through winding paths and vines that tease,
A hedgehog juggles with the bees.
Each thorny twig curls up with glee,
As laughter floats like a melody.

A turtle with shades moves slow and grand,
While fireflies twinkle as the band.
The bushes hum a tune so spry,
As whispers ripple gently by.

A playful skunk dons a bold parade,
While critters gather in this charade.
Flowers snap their petals in cheer,
At every giggle, no one shows fear.

So let the tale of nature's play,
Remind us to frolic in a fun way.
With thorns that pinch and stories to share,
In this world of whimsy, joy awaits there.

Wit Among the Thickets

In thickets deep, the jesters roam,
Each critter finding a way back home.
A chattering squirrel shares a jest,
While bees take notes, they're on a quest.

An otter slips with grace and flair,
As laughter ripples in the air.
Even the rocks have tales to tell,
Of mishaps and giggles, all is well.

The moonlight casts a playful glow,
While badgers rhyme, putting on a show.
A windy breeze joins in the fun,
Whispering jokes 'til the night is done.

So wander in where the wild winds play,
And let your worries just drift away.
Among the thickets, let laughter swell,
For in this world, all is well.

Whispers in the Wildwood

In the thicket, squirrels schemed,
Chasing shadows, wild and dreamed,
A fox with flair, a tale to tell,
Danced through whispers, all was well.

A patch of mushrooms, quite a sight,
Mushroom caps in a silly fight,
They wobbled left, they swayed right,
In the tangle, pure delight.

A nimble hare, with a quirky grin,
Played hopscotch where the bushes thin,
With every leap, a chuckle bright,
Laughter echoes through the night.

Beneath the moon, the jests arise,
Fireflies flicker like friendly spies,
In the wildwood, joy's our treasure,
Nature's jest, our simple pleasure.

Thicket of Chatter

In the thicket, where secrets bloom,
A parrot squawks with much costume,
Tales of mischief, his voice so bold,
In feathery shades of bright and gold.

A raccoon with a laugh so sly,
Dug through trash, oh my, oh my!
With a hat made of leaves, he pranced around,
Chasing giggles from the ground.

The crickets chirp in rhythmic tune,
As frogs croak out their silly croon,
A melody of mischief shared,
Where nature's humor is prepared.

Through tangled vines, the jokes will sway,
Turning night into a playful day,
With the stars above, we find our way,
In laughter's grip, we love to stay.

Jests Among the Vines

Amidst the vines, a spider weaves,
A tapestry of trickster leaves,
She plays a game of hide and seek,
While beetles laugh, they squeak and peek.

A clumsy calf, with wobbly legs,
Stomps through bushes, breaking pegs,
His bovine buddy rolls in glee,
Tail wagging wildly, oh, what a spree!

The wind joins in, with a cheeky breeze,
Tickling noses, bending trees,
As whispers whirl in nature's hall,
Every rustle, a jest from all.

So let us play in this merry glade,
Where laughter blooms and fears will fade,
With every vine, a new delight,
In jovial echoes, we unite.

Twisted Tangents

In a maze of twists, the critters roam,
A possum makes this place his home,
With a swagger, he trips on air,
Cackles follow, it's quite a stare.

A goat on a path, quite the sight,
Challenges shadows to a fun fight,
With an acorn crown, he takes the lead,
As laughter dances around with speed.

Silly squirrels debate the day,
Who's the best in this chic ballet?
Their chatter's wild, hearts feel so light,
In twisted paths, all wrongs feel right.

Through the green chaos, jests will unfurl,
Each quirk a gem in nature's swirl,
The humor thrives, with absence of care,
In this playful world, we share and dare.

Jest and Jumble

In the garden, where chaos rules,
Squirrels chatter, and tease like fools.
A dog chases shadows, on a whim,
While flowers giggle, edges dim.

A cat plays king, on a sunlit throne,
With paws of mischief, he claims his own.
The gnomes whisper secrets, behind the weeds,
In a world where laughter is all that it needs.

With a hop and a skip, the rabbits dance,
While weeds weave stories, as if by chance.
A parrot squawks jokes, from a branch up high,
In the jumbled mix, the fun can't die.

So let's join the frolic, in this lively spree,
Where nature's jesters beckon you and me.
In a realm of quirk, let's lose the norm,
And bathe in laughter, as spirits warm.

Fleeting Fronds

Whispers in the wind, the leaves rejoice,
As laughter escapes, the trees make noise.
A beetle in glasses, reading the news,
Critiques the weather, with silly views.

Dancing ferns, with their floppy tails,
Join in a gossip of love and fails.
The sun peeks through, with a cheeky grin,
While the daisies plot, to pull a prank or spin.

A snail's slow waltz, it's quite the show,
With timing so poor, but energy to glow.
The pond's fish giggle, as they flip and flop,
In bright colored scales, they can't seem to stop.

Join this parade of whimsy divine,
Where every leaf holds a beer, and wine.
In fleeting moments, we shed our facade,
And dance in the frenzy, feeling quite odd.

Frolics in the Foliage

In the tangled shade, the critters scheme,
A rabbit with quirks, and a mischievous dream.
He wears a top hat, and twirls on the grass,
While the hedgehog takes bets on who'll fall, alas!

Laughter bursts forth from thicket and vine,
As owls trade quips while sipping on thyme.
The wisecracking crow steals a shine,
With jokes so dry, they blur the line.

A dance of the ants, in perfect time,
They perform for the bees, just sublime.
While flowers roll their petals in glee,
In this wild performance, all feel so free.

So come join the fun, in the leafy expanse,
Where chaos rules, and all creatures prance.
With a skip and a hop, we embrace the thrill,
In a world full of quirks, let's laugh at will.

Echoes of Ivy

Beneath the arches, the ivy climbs high,
While whispers of laughter float through the sky.
A chameleon sings, in colors so bright,
His serenade echoes, a comical sight.

Old trees share tales of their many years,
With roots deep in jokes and leaves soaked in cheers.
The squirrels play tag, on branches they race,
In this woodland circus, they find their space.

Mice in tuxedos, waltzing with flair,
While daisies decide to straighten their hair.
The moon peeks down, with a wink and a sigh,
As laughter reverberates, letting joy fly.

So revel in this, the nature's tight knit,
Where humor and mischief perfectly sit.
In echoes of ivy, let whimsy take flight,
In this funny garden, everything's bright.

Mirth Amongst the Foliage

In the garden, weeds take stage,
Twisting tales like gossip's page.
A tumble here, a laugh shared wide,
With every step, we slip and glide.

The flowers giggle, swaying light,
As butterflies join in the fright.
"Who's the fairest?" blooms declare,
While bees debate without a care.

In vines that tangle, jokes are spun,
Each prickly stem, a crafty pun.
Laughter echoes through leafy beds,
While muddy boots seek fun instead.

So cheer arises, wild and free,
In this patch of hilarity.
The sun shines down, a playful gaze,
As nature laughs in sunny rays.

Jive with the Jumble

Amongst the chaos, jumps a sprite,
A twist of humor, pure delight.
With tangled limbs, we dance around,
In this goofy patch of ground.

The knotted branches try to tease,
A playful jab, a gentle squeeze.
With every step, we bump and spin,
In this wild chase, we wear a grin.

A secret whisper in the breeze,
As laughter comes with such great ease.
We'll jive along, through thick and thin,
Entwined in fun, let's dive right in!

So skip and hop through tangled trails,
As giggles echo, joy prevails.
In every mess, there's something spry,
Just join the jive, you'll learn to fly!

Skirmishes of Style

In fancy raiments, critters battle,
With flashy hats, they prance and rattle.
"I'm the chicest beast!" one claims with flair,
While leggings snag on branches bare.

Headlines swirl in leafy shakes,
As squirrels strut and do their pranks.
Each furry friend dons quite the getup,
But who can top the funky pup?

A wild debate on twiggy trends,
As laughter fills where style transcends.
With tangled tails, they vie for grace,
Each claiming top spot in this wild race.

So strut your stuff, let fashion reign,
In this laughter, we share the gain.
For in this throng of quirky threads,
True style is found where fun spreads!

Crooked Conversations

In corners curled, where shadows play,
Whispers dance in disarray.
With vines entwined, they share a jest,
While petals blush at every jest.

A chat about the sun and rain,
Takes twists and turns, yet feels quite plain.
"You should have seen the size of that!"
A tale grows taller, now imagine that!

The tangled stories weave and wind,
With every laugh, new truths combined.
A crooked path through blooming cheer,
Where friendships bloom, and none feel fear.

So gather close, and lean on me,
In each odd chat, we find the key.
For every quirk and laugh we find,
Creates a bond that leaves us blind.

Thicket Tales and Mirth

In the wild where the hedges giggle,
Squirrels argue in a comical wiggle.
A rabbit hops in a silly parade,
While a fox makes a jest, quite unafraid.

The bushes chuckle, their leaves all a-shiver,
As a snail dreams of bright ponds to deliver.
Each gnat flutters by, a tiny comedian,
Painting the day in a quirky median.

A turtle's slow waltz brings laughs from the crew,
While the bees buzz a tune, oddly askew.
The wind plays a trick, tosses hats in the air,
Nature's own dance with humor laid bare.

So gather round, let the stories unwind,
In the thicket of joy, pure fun intertwined.
With mischief and giggles, the hours flit by,
In the heart of the thicket, we laugh till we cry.

The Playful Grapevine

Twisting and turning, the vines seem to giggle,
Sharing secrets in a cheerful wiggle.
A raccoon in a hat, quite the sight to behold,
Tells tales of the nights when the moon's made of gold.

The grapes roll their eyes, oh, such silly pranks,
While the birds lend their voices in merry planks.
With beaks full of jokes, they chirp without pause,
As ladybugs vie for the coveted applause.

A swing from a branch sends the squirrels in glee,
As butterflies dance with a buzzing decree.
Each leaf drops down, a comedic retreat,
In a festival of laughter, so wild and sweet.

So join in the mirth where the green laughter lives,
In the playful embrace that the vineyard gives.
With sunshine and cheer, let's tumble and race,
In the vineyard of jests, we find our place.

Humor in the Garden of Shadows

In the nooks where the daylight softly fades,
Green sprites are at work, making funny charades.
A gopher with glasses, so clever and spry,
Recites comical tales to the clouds passing by.

The lilies throw shade, oh such playful remarks,
While the shadows do tango, dancing like larks.
A hedgehog in bow ties, the main act of the show,
Steals laughs from the night with his charming faux pas.

The moon chuckles bright with a glimmering jest,
As crickets take turns in their comedic quest.
Beneath the tall trees, a riddle unfolds,
As the garden's proud secrets are humorously told.

Embrace the odd moments where laughter is sown,
In shadows of gardens, where humor is grown.
With giggles and snorts, let your spirit take flight,
In this whimsical place, where all feels just right.

Jestful Twine of Nature

Between tangled roots, the laughter does sprout,
As clever little critters convene for a spout.
A wise old owl hoots, offering quips,
While rabbits roll over, lost in their slips.

The sun flickers down, playing hide and seek,
As a badger spins tales in a voice so unique.
The flowers burst forth, sharing puns with a smile,
While the laughter of frogs lingers all the while.

A kite caught in branches, flapping with flair,
Brings giggles and grins to the creatures who care.
With mock-serious tones, the trees join the fun,
As whispers of joy in the breeze softly run.

So roam through the forest, let laughter ignite,
In the jestful twine, embrace pure delight.
Together we'll frolic in nature's embrace,
Where humor unravels and spirits interlace.

Cheeky Sprouts

Tiny leaves in playful dance,
They giggle in the breeze's prance.
With sprightly hops, they tease the air,
Distracting folks with leafy flair.

A dandelion joins the jest,
Soon tangled in a leafy fest.
Laughter echoes through the green,
As plants unite in joyful sheen.

With roots that wiggle, stems that sway,
They plot their fun from day to day.
Each raindrop brings a chance for glee,
In this wild plant community.

When shadows fall, they start to pluck,
In the moonlight, they press their luck.
A prank or two, a twist or knot,
Those cheeky sprouts have all the plot.

Merriment in the Moss

In fuzzy patches, laughter grows,
Underneath the shady throes.
The little critters share a joke,
As mushrooms giggle 'neath the cloak.

A squirrel tripping on his tail,
Fumbling through the leafy trail.
He laughs and rolls in soft, dank grace,
While hidden creatures take their place.

Here, tales of folly soon unfold,
With whispers softly retold.
Amidst the green, a festive cheer,
In every nook, there's fun to hear.

As twilight drapes its evening light,
The mossy stage gleams in delight.
With critters primed for nightly jest,
A rollicking ball in nature's nest.

Mischief Among the Beasts

The raccoon plots a clever scheme,
With nuts concealed, a flashy dream.
He winks at friends, then makes his dash,
A furry blur through shrubs that clash.

The hedgehog snickers, rolling by,
Playing tricks with a playful sigh.
With tiny quills and cheeky sneers,
He revels in the fun that steers.

A wise old owl hoots from his perch,
Surveying all, with a wise-bird lurch.
While creatures scheme in joyous flood,
In tangled brush, they share their good.

When nighttime calls, they'll gather near,
To spin old tales, to laugh, to cheer.
For mischief blooms with every night,
These beasts of fun all take flight.

Shimmers of Humor

In shades of green, the sunlight glints,
Where laughter weaves through all the hints.
With petals bright, and jokes to spin,
A dance begins, let fun begin.

The bumblebee buzzes in delight,
Tickling blooms, what a funny sight!
While ladybugs in pairs will glide,
They share a wink, their joy can't hide.

Each blade of grass, a subtle laugh,
Reflects the sun, that merry craft.
In every nook, in shadows cast,
There's humor lingering, unsurpassed.

As twilight falls, stars twinkle gleam,
In nature's realm where giggles beam.
With every rustle, a punchline flares,
In this lively patch, joy always shares.

Shadows of Humor

In the wild where laughter plays,
Critters giggle on summer days.
A squirrel with a nutty grin,
Teases all the folks who spin.

The hedgehog donned a tiny hat,
Danced around, oh what a spat!
While rabbits with their twitchy ears,
Share cheeky tales, dispelling fears.

A chase ensues through leafy lanes,
As friends lace puns like old refrain.
A ticklish breeze begins to swirl,
As mischief secrets start to twirl.

In each shadow, a giggle roams,
Where every creature feels like home.
With quirks and laughter intertwined,
Nature's joy is well-defined.

Riddles in the Greenery

Amidst the leaves, a riddle springs,
From chattering birds, such silly things.
A worm in glasses solves the plot,
While snails debate what they forgot.

The oak tree leans in, winks a grin,
As flowers prance and sway within.
Can you hear the puns on the breeze?
Nature's humor, sure to tease.

In twisted vines, a joke takes shape,
As vines entwine, our minds escape.
A ladybug cracks a joke so sly,
While caterpillars laugh and sigh.

With every branch a playful jest,
In quiet nooks, they find their rest.
In whispers of the green around,
The heart of mirth is always found.

Playful Thorns

In hedges green, a mischief brews,
With twinkling eyes and playful views.
A thistle laughs, "I'm not so sharp!"
While daisies strum a bloom-filled harp.

The rose winks and shows a thorn,
While joking 'bout the day they're born.
In secret chats beneath the sky,
The blooms crack jokes and let them fly.

Around the bends the laughter spills,
With quirky tales of blooms and chills.
In tangled vines, they share delight,
A comic twist in morning light.

Nature chuckles, a joyous song,
As thorns and petals dance along.
With every poke, a story spins,
Where laughter lives, and joy begins.

Quirks of the Thicket

Within the thicket, secrets hide,
Where critters frolic, side by side.
A fox dons specs to read the news,
As laughter springs from every muse.

The bushes hum, a lively tune,
While crafty crows plot 'neath the moon.
With whispers shared and jesting glances,
They leap and bound in playful dances.

An owl misreads, "Who's there?" he cries,
While hedgehogs nudge with knowing sighs.
In silly stunts, they take their aim,
In this wild world, who's really tame?

In every nook, a chuckle waits,
As friendship blooms and fun creates.
Among the quirks and quirky pranks,
The thicket sparkles, as laughter ranks.

Sprouts of Silliness

Beneath a bush so brazenly wide,
A squirrel in shades thinks he's the pride.
He dances around, so light on his feet,
But trips on a twig - oh, what a defeat!

The robin nearby can't help but caw,
As the ground shakes softly from his great flaw.
With giggles and chirps, the forest takes part,
In a comedy scene that warms every heart.

A rabbit hops in, with buck teeth so bright,
He joins the parade, spreading laughs through the night.
With cada step, he wiggles and jives,
While all other critters, in chuckles, arrive.

So come join this romp, where the tea flows like cheer,
Laughter and joy are the guests we hold dear.
As the sun dips low, painting skies a soft hue,
The forest sings on with laughter anew.

Caps of Chortles

In a hat shop run by a quirky old crow,
Each cap he creates has its own little glow.
With feathers and ruffles, and ribbons galore,
He tosses them high, while they all hit the floor.

A fox struts in, with a twist to his tail,
Says, "Give me a cap that will never turn pale!"
The crow just cackles, "That's quite a tall ask,
But here's one for giggles; just put on this mask!"

With a wink and a grin, the fox takes the plunge,
Then bursts into laughter, he's ready to lunge.
As friends gather 'round for a party so grand,
Caps fly through the air, a whimsical band.

They dance on the grass, in a merriment spree,
Each cap telling tales, as wild as can be!
Laughter erupts, joy fills the whole land,
In this hat-tastic moment, all folly is planned.

Tones from the Twists

With spirals and curves, this place has a vibe,
Where paths twist and twirl, life's a joyous jibe.
A hedgehog rolls in, with a horn made of cheese,
Declaring, "Join in, if you dare, if you please!"

A band of small creatures, they gather and cheer,
Each note they produce is like music to hear.
A tune full of gaggles, each pitch makes them chuckle,
As laughter erupts in a jubilant bubble.

The wind starts to dance, wrapping all in its glee,
With whispers of fun 'neath the old sycamore tree.
A badger in boots prances right to the beat,
"More cheese for the show, now that's quite the treat!"

So spin through the twists, let the music unite,
In a world painted bright with humor's delight.
As laughter spins 'round in a whimsical loop,
Life's a grand jig in this cheery old troupe.

Laughing Leaves

In a grove full of greens, a giggle persists,
With each rustling sound, nature quietly twists.
The leaves share secrets, they sway to a tune,
A wacky performance, right under the moon.

A chipmunk, quite proud in a coat made of fluff,
Tells tales of the days when the weather was tough.
He recalls how he slipped on a juicy old nut,
And tumbled right down, what a marvelous strut!

The branches all creak, in a symphony fine,
As critters join in, with a wink and a shine.
"Let's roll with the fun; let's dance through the night,
These leaves give us joy, make our worries take flight!"

So dance in this grove, as the laughter grows loud,
Each chuckle a treasure, in nature we're proud.
With each little rustle, a cheer fills the air,
In a world wrapped in whimsy, all troubles lay bare.

Grapple of Wit

In a garden of giggles, weeds run wild,
A rogue snail slips, his humor compiled.
Laughter springs from petals bright,
As jests take flight in morning light.

A hedgehog grins with a quill-hat twist,
While squirrels plot in a nutty mist.
Wit flows free like the springtime air,
Each chuckle tickles without a care.

In leafy shadows, jokes are spun,
As lazy bees dance; the real fun.
They buzz around in playful jest,
A buzzing band; their humor's the best.

So grab a friend and join the mix,
In the backyard drama of silly tricks.
Let every thorn tell a story bright,
In the gleeful game of wit and light.

Twine and Tease

Underneath the tangled vines,
Chickens chuckle, dropping lines.
A rabbit hops with a cheeky grin,
While a mischievous fox spins to win.

The crows caw secrets on the breeze,
While the sun dips low, bringing ease.
A dance of shadows, teases collide,
As giggles rumble from every side.

With slippery words and playful nips,
The garden's alive with jokes and quips.
A tortoise jokes on a mossy throne,
While crickets strum in a jovial tone.

So gather and grin in the tangled maze,
Where laughter sparks in the sun's warm rays.
When playtime calls in the evening's delight,
Let whimsy twine in the fading light.

Echoes of Merriment

In a thicket where giggles bloom,
A raccoon stumbles, clears the gloom.
With a wink, he falls into a patch,
Of daisies that dance in a joyful match.

The frogs croak rhythms, a silly tune,
While fireflies flicker under the moon.
They ribbit and jive, a lively crew,
Turning the night into revelry new.

From mossy stones, laughter springs,
As playful neighbors flap their wings.
The echoes bounce in a vibrant flight,
Carrying joy until morning light.

So join the fun, don't be shy,
In this merry world, let spirits fly.
Each chuckled tale a vibrant thread,
Weaving gales of laughter, joy widespread.

Jesting in the Jungle

Swinging monkeys toss their quips,
While toucans share their snappy scripts.
In this wild realm, no time for frowns,
Just playful banter from furry clowns.

A sloth tells tales at a leisurely pace,
With giggles shared in a leafy embrace.
Each shade cradles a joke or two,
As the sounds of cheer break right on through.

The jaguar lounges, a king in disguise,
While the parrot imitates silly cries.
With bunny hops and fluttering wings,
Laughter richly flows, as joyfulness springs.

In this verdant hub, jesters abound,
With chuckles echoing all around.
So swing along and join the spree,
In the jungle's fun, where we all can be.

Whimsy in the Woods

In a thicket alive with cheer,
Squirrels plot from far and near.
With acorns in their crafty paws,
They laugh at nature's little flaws.

A wobbly rabbit tries to hop,
But trips and lands with quite a plop.
The deer all snicker, quite unkind,
As the raccoons roll and unwind.

The sunbeams dance on leafy floors,
While chipmunks giggle through the doors.
They share a joke, a cheeky jest,
In this woodland where they jest.

Laughter echoes through each glade,
Where every creature joins the parade.
Nature's laughter fills the air,
Whimsy reigns without a care.

Frivolous Flora

Petals wobble with delight,
As flowers chat from morn til night.
Tulips tease the stubborn bees,
Who bumble round, just trying to please.

Daisies whisper silly tunes,
While toes tap 'neath the laughing moons.
Buttercups roll on the grassy spree,
Chasing dreams of a honeyed sea.

The roses boast of vibrant grace,
As violets play the shyest face.
A daffodil, in joyful thrall,
Sings to the wind, declaring all.

Nature's jesters wear their crowns,
In a kingdom made of gowns.
Each petal shares a light-hearted rhyme,
Where giggles bloom, lost in time.

Hilarity in the Hedge

In the hedges, mischief brews,
With tiny creatures swapping views.
A hedgehog's quill gets stuck in jest,
While mice trade tales, they're feeling blessed.

A tortoise, slow, but wise and spry,
Makes quips that make the critters cry.
His shell, a shield of laughter's art,
As he spins jokes upon his cart.

The wrens chirp tales of daring feats,
While busy ants march on their beats.
Each corner hides a snicker or cheer,
A rummaged laugh more precious here.

Beneath the leaves a party grows,
As hedgehogs share their funny woes.
In this shrubbery, the jokes unfold,
A merry kangaroo, or so I'm told.

Tides of Tangle

In the mess where vines entwine,
Frogs croak rhythms, quite divine.
The snappy beats, a croaky band,
Croaking up a wiggly stand.

Crickets chirp a silly tune,
Underneath a wobbly moon.
With every hop, they dance with glee,
A tangled jest of jubilee.

A bevy of buzzers spin away,
On a breeze that loves to play.
The ladybugs chuckle, turning bright,
As the thistles join the flight.

Nature's joy is all around,
In jumbled threads, laughter found.
With silly antics everywhere,
The tides of tangle seem to care.

Laughing with the Boughs

In the shade of the trees, we jest and we play,
Twisting our words in a mischievous way.
With laughter that rings through the dappled light,
Each quip and each giggle takes glorious flight.

Squirrels are busy, their chatter so loud,
While we share our tales, feeling quite proud.
A woodpecker drums out a beat so absurd,
We follow the rhythm, each silly word.

A parrot swings by with a wink and a tease,
He mimics our laughter, puts us at ease.
With every distraction, we dance like a breeze,
Joy echoes around us, as sweet as the peas.

As shadows grow long and the sun starts to fade,
We settle our bets from the games that we played.
With smiles on our faces and hearts full of cheer,
We leave with the leaves, our tales held dear.

Quips Among the Twigs

Underneath the branches, we gather with glee,
Trading our jokes like it's a grand spree.
A twig snaps beneath us, we both start to laugh,
Imagining it's part of our clever craft.

A rabbit hops by with a cheeky little grin,
Joining our revels, letting the fun begin.
We pass around giggles like treasures unshared,
Each punchline delivered, impeccably paired.

The shadows are dancing; the owls look bemused,
At how so much laughter can feel so infused.
As crickets join in with their rhythmic chirps,
Our cheerful brigade makes a colorful circus.

As twilight closes in and our voices grow hushed,
With the day's jolly jests, our hearts are now flushed.
We scatter like leaves on an upswept breeze,
Covered in humor, our joy never flees.

Jests in the Wildwood

In the wildwood laughing, our spirits take flight,
With jests that resound from morning till night.
A chipmunk joins in, making all of us grin,
Telling tall tales of nut wars he's been in.

The breeze whispers secrets, so cunning, so sly,
As we stand there and marvel at jokes flying high.
Dancing through foliage, we take quite a chance,
With each clever punchline, we all start to prance.

A fox with a smirk adds his comedic flair,
As laughter wells up, spilling sweetly through air.
We toast to our folly with cups made of leaves,
Celebrating every wild quip that we weave.

As the stars overhead begin twinkling bright,
We wrap up our frolic, bringing day to night.
With hearts filled with laughter, we bid the woods cheer,
Until the next time we gather in here.

Echoes of the Murmuring Leaves

Beneath the green canopy, giggles collide,
As whispers of humor in shadows reside.
The leaves start to giggle, the branches all sway,
Echoing laughter that brightens the day.

A raccoon with mischief scurries on by,
He trips on his paws, oh my, oh my!
With a cheeky grin, he lifts up his hat,
As if to say, 'What was wrong with that?'

Beneath arching canopies of vibrant green hue,
We swap silly stories, an old and a new.
With bright eyes aglow and hearts full of light,
The warmth of our laughter makes everything right.

As dusk turns to darkness, our voices take flight,
In echoes of joy that linger through night.
With the moon as our witness, under stars high above,
We stand as a chorus of friendship and love.

The Jesting Hedge

In a thicket of quirks, a prankster lies,
With scarlet berries and mischievous eyes.
Tickling the leaves, a giggle takes flight,
As the bushes conspire to cause a delight.

A squirrel in costume, a hat far too grand,
Dances like royalty, a sight so unplanned.
The jests ripen sweetly on branches of green,
While the wind whispers secrets, unheard, unseen.

Beneath the green canopy, laughter is found,
Where shadows are painted with humor abound.
Thorns bear a grin, they chuckle and tease,
As the sunbeams bounce off with whimsical ease.

So gather your chuckles, come join this grand show,
Where the prickle of folly encourages grow.
The jesting hedge beckons with playful intrigue,
A riddle of laughter, the heart's joyous league.

Laughter in the Underbrush

In the undergrowth thick, where the critters convene,
A chorus of giggles, both raucous and keen.
A rabbit in slippers hops past with a grin,
While a fox throws a party, to lure all within.

With beanstalks for microphones, crickets play tunes,
The moon winks in rhythm, aflutter with prunes.
They dance on the mushrooms, all toes and all tails,
As fireflies wink in their glittering gales.

A wise old toad croaks the latest of jokes,
While beneath his green belly, the laughter evokes.
Every chuckle a whisper, a tickle in night,
As shadows join in, adding jest to the light.

So tiptoe through this realm, where humor's in bloom,
And leave all your worries beneath the green gloom.
For in the underbrush, hearty laughter will reign,
Where the echoes of joy erase all the mundane.

Witty Twists of the Wild

Where the forest unfolds with a twist and a jest,
Creatures conspire in a life of the blessed.
A skunk dons a mask, declares himself king,
While the squirrels vote 'YES' to everything.

A gathering frenzy of feathers and fur,
In a comical clash, the antics confer.
A crow makes a riddle that's silly yet grand,
And a hedgehog with puns delivers on demand.

Every vine tells a story, each branch has a plot,
With humor embedded in all that they've got.
A laugh like a melody scattered with glee,
In the wild, every chuckle is wild and free.

So venture this way, if you seek to unwind,
With the witty and jolly, bright spirits combined.
The torments of seriousness fade in the day,
In the twists of the wild, we find joy on the way.

Echoes of the Forest Frolic

In the hush of the woods, where the echoes do play,
Laughter unfurls in a carefree ballet.
A moose wears a scarf, with a smile so wide,
While beavers are scheming a splashy slide.

With whispers of giggles that tickle the trees,
As raccoons don capes, dancing light in the breeze.
The owls hoot their laughter, wise wisdom in tune,
Crafting jests in the twilight, beneath the full moon.

Every flower a friend, with petals of cheer,
As the chuckles entwine in the fresh morning air.
The forest transforms with a whimsy so rare,
Every nook holds a punchline, a quip, a flair.

So wander through wilds where the humor is rife,
And let the sweet echoes bring laughter to life.
For in every rustle, every light-hearted call,
Lives the spirit of fun, inviting us all.

Gossamer Threads of Humor

In the garden where shadows play,
A witty squirrel steals the day,
With acorns tossed like joke confetti,
Nature laughs, it's never petty.

A fox in socks does somersaults,
While rabbits giggle at his faults,
A butterfly winks, spreading cheer,
Whispering jokes that all can hear.

The breeze joins in, its voice a tease,
Rustling leaves with giggly ease,
A chorus of chuckles fills the air,
As laughter blooms everywhere.

So dance with glee, let spirits soar,
In this haven, there's always more,
With smiles woven in sunlit threads,
Where joy abounds and laughter spreads.

Joking Among the Thickets

In tangled vines where critters dwell,
The hedgehogs spin their funny spell,
Telling tales of daring escape,
While crickets croon in playful shape.

A wise old owl with a knowing gaze,
Mocks the goofiness in the haze,
While fireflies wink like tiny stars,
Sharing secrets behind the bars.

A porcupine with quills so bright,
Says, "Life's a prickly, funny sight!"
And all around, the laughter glows,
As petals dance, and wisecracks flow.

So explore the thickets, take a chance,
Join the creatures in their dance,
For humor hides where we least expect,
In nature's thickets, joy's perfect.

Giggles Beneath the Canopy

Beneath the trees where shadows blend,
A gnome is plotting, chasing trends,
With mushrooms sprouting jokes so sly,
As squirrels stifle giggles nearby.

A chattering jay thinks it's quite smart,
With puns that tickle every heart,
While mushrooms puff, puffing air,
Spreading laughter everywhere.

The brook hums low, a funny tune,
While frogs in hats croak at the moon,
A forest full of silly sounds,
Where joy and mischief often abound.

So linger long beneath the trees,
Join in the jest, enjoy the breeze,
For life is sweet, with laughs we share,
In nature's embrace, we find our flair.

Nature's Playful Prickles

In the patch where the daisies grin,
A hedgehog spins, it's where we begin,
With mischievous quips and prancy feats,
While laughter twirls on tiny feet.

A snake in a hat slinks with flair,
Its jokes leave all in a humorous stare,
While bumblebees buzz a tune so jolly,
Filling the air with buzz and folly.

The winds weave tales of silliness grand,
As critters join in, hand in hand,
Each twig a stage for laughter's dance,
Where smiles bloom and hearts entrance.

So come and play where the wild things are,
In nature's realm, we'll wander far,
For with each chuckle, the world grows bright,
In prickly patches, we find delight.

Chit and Chortle

In the garden, whispers fly,
As laughter dances, oh so spry.
A squirrel snickers, twirls around,
While petals tumble to the ground.

The gnome wears shades, a sly old grin,
He's heard the tales of win and sin.
Fragrant jokes in the summer air,
Tickling noses with flair and care.

The daisies giggle, roots in tow,
They wiggle-waggle, putting on a show.
Bees buzz by, with chuckles sweet,
As wildflowers sway to the beat.

Underneath the sun's warm glow,
Crisp quips bubble, in a row.
In this plot of green, we take our stand,
With mirthful giggles, hand in hand.

Wild and Witty

In the thicket, fun takes flight,
A fox darts past, oh what a sight!
With every dash, a joke is spun,
A cheeky grin, the day is won.

A parrot squawks, sharing a jest,
He's claimed the crown, a feathered pest.
With flapping wings, he steals the scene,
Chasing shadows, bright and keen.

Frogs croak out their silly tunes,
Underneath the winking moons.
A trombone frog plays on the log,
As the night wraps round like a fog.

In this chaos where laughter reigns,
Every leaf seems to entertain.
With nature's charm, we find delight,
In the wild's embrace, we laugh so bright.

Catching the Light

Sunbeams scatter through the trees,
While fireflies dance with playful ease.
A wink from nature, a chuckle so bright,
Catching moments in the gentle light.

Bumblebees buzz in rhythmic haste,
Sharing secrets with sweetened taste.
In this sunny, lively spree,
A chorus sings, just wait and see.

The flutter of wings, a feathered jest,
Each tiny spark, a silly quest.
Leaves rustle laughter, soft and slight,
In this tapestry, everything feels right.

With every shadow, giggles unfold,
As sunlight threads through stories told.
In this playful realm where we unite,
We gather joy from catching the light.

Gleeful Entanglements

Tangled vines play hide and seek,
While laughter ripples through the creek.
A squirrel quips from a lofty height,
With acorn hats and pure delight.

A gnarled tree shares its wise old tunes,
Bowing low to the whims of moons.
With knots and twirls, a silly spree,
As whispers twine in harmony.

Each rustling leaf is a giggling friend,
In this merry mess that has no end.
The breezes tease, like playful sprites,
Sending shivers of joyful delights.

In these entangled tales we weave,
A tapestry of fun to believe.
With every chuckle, we take our chance,
To dance and laugh in the wild expanse.

Cheerful Clashes

In a garden where the weeds all play,
A squirrel tripped on a bright bouquet.
With a cheeky grin, it made its dash,
Only to land in a merry splash.

A snail winked at a passing bee,
"You won't outrun me, just wait and see!"
The bee buzzed back, a taunt on the air,
"You're slow as molasses, I just don't care!"

Petunias giggled at the grand show,
As the ants carried crumbs, moving slow.
The hedgehog chuckled, behind the fence,
"Now that's humor—so dense, so intense!"

With laughter echoing throughout the scene,
The garden bloomed in a joyous routine.
Each bumble and brush, a hilarious act,
Nature's own play, a whimsical pact.

Mirthful Murmurs

In a thicket where shadows tossed,
A fox danced away, but it nearly lost.
Caught on a bramble, it gave a squeak,
For all its swagger, it felt quite weak.

A mouse nearby found the scene grand,
With tiny giggles that echoed 'round the land.
"Do show some grace," it whispered with glee,
As the fox turned redder than a cherry tree.

A butterfly flitted, teasing the fox,
"What's your fancy? A dance or a box?"
The fox retorted, "I'll take the stage,
If laughter's the prize, let's engage!"

The woods erupted in cheerful hoots,
As critters revealed their hidden pursuits.
Nature's jesters sparkled with charm,
In mirthful whispers, there's never harm.

Serendipity in the Shrubbery

Among the leaves, a duo conspired,
A lizard and frog, both quite inspired.
They plotted a trick on a flock of small birds,
With giggles and plans, like jumbled words.

"Let's hide in the moss, quick, take your place!"
The lizard exclaimed with a grin on its face.
The frogs croaked loudly, distracting the flock,
As the lizard snickered, just behind a rock.

But the birds, quite savvy, caught onto their game,
They chirped and flew off, ignoring the fame.
"Too clever by half," croaked the frog with a sigh,
As their antics just fluttered and waved goodbye!

Yet laughter echoed where mischief was sown,
In the brush, where secrets were playfully thrown.
With every flop and each tumble and twist,
It's the joy of the chase that cannot be missed.

Lively Larks

A pair of old cats played a rowdy tune,
With paw taps and purrs, they danced 'neath the moon.
Their energy soared as they swirled about,
Amidst the tall grass, with playful shout.

A raccoon swung by, holding snacks in a bag,
"Can I join the fun? Or are you all that rag?"
"No snacks while we jig, that's the little rule!"
The cats replied, acting the fool.

So the raccoon just laughed and jumped in the fray,
With steps so absurd, it stole the display.
They tumbled and rolled, a sight so surreal,
Creating a whirl of joy they could feel.

With twinkling stars casting light on their play,
Their laughter resounded, brightening the way.
In the heart of the night, where wild spirits soar,
Life's little joys open nature's door.

Glee in the Bramble Patch

In a thicket where laughter grows,
Critters converse in curious flows.
A hedgehog wears a tiny hat,
While birds gossip over a chat.

Mice dance wildly without a care,
Tails entwined in the freshened air.
Squirrels jest with acorn tricks,
Each punchline lands with joyous clicks.

A rabbit tells a tale so grand,
Of mischief played across the land.
The sun shines bright on their parade,
In a wild world where joy is made.

Together they find joy without fuss,
In tangled weeds and lots of thrust.
With cheerfulness, they roam about,
In their patch of giggles, there's no doubt.

Twists of Joy

In a corner where smiles appear,
Playful jibes are all we hear.
The wind whispers secrets so sweet,
As critters gather for a treat.

A cat pretends to be quite sly,
While a mouse scurries, oh my, oh my!
Their banter dances in the breeze,
Tickling hearts with gentle tease.

A toad jumps high, a pratfall king,
With croaks that make the chorus sing.
Every flip and every flop,
Brings a chuckle, makes them stop.

In their haven of mirthful glee,
Joy's the bond between you and me.
With every twist and turn they share,
They find pure laughter everywhere.

Chatter in the Wilds

Underneath the shady boughs,
Nature's laughter takes its vows.
A fox slips by with a crafty grin,
While a chicken tells tales of when.

Hopping here and flapping there,
Even bees join in the air.
With giggles bright and winks so sly,
The forest echoes as voices fly.

A mischievous crow caws with zest,
While a bear claims he's the best.
But wait! A turtle's slow retort,
Leaves them gasping in funny sport.

In this wild world of playful cheer,
Every chatter draws friends near.
With snickers shared and laughter bright,
The wilds are filled with pure delight.

Lively Twists

Amidst the twists of nature's spree,
Frogs leap forth with urgency.
While bees buzz tunes that tickle the skin,
Each turn brings a smile from within.

Bunnies play hopscotch by the brook,
Drawing glances from every nook.
A wise old owl offers a joke,
His laughter spreads like friendly smoke.

A chase ensues with giggles galore,
As critters tumble, dance, and soar.
With every twist and turn they take,
Joy's the comeback for good times' sake.

In this realm of winding ways,
Laughter reigns for all their days.
With fringe and frolic at play, you see,
A tapestry woven of pure glee.

Smirks amongst the Shrubs

In the thicket, whispers fly,
Sneaky squirrels, tails held high.
Jokes exchange in leafy halls,
Laughter bursts as nature calls.

A hedgehog winks, a rabbit grins,
Ticklish vines share silly spins.
Each twist and turn, a giggle found,
While underneath, the secrets bound.

The wind joins in with a playful sigh,
Rustling leaves, oh my, oh my!
They dance around, both shy and bold,
These jovial tales, in green, retold.

Amidst the shrubs, mirth takes place,
Every creature, a funny face.
With nature's jest, we trot about,
In this patch, there's never doubt.

Jolly Twists

Twisted branches, a cheeky sight,
Chirpy birds take silly flight.
Frolicking winds throw leaves around,
Giggling grass beneath the ground.

A turtle slips in a muddy plot,
While frogs cheer on, with giddy sport.
Laughter echoes through the glade,
As nature's pranks are slyly played.

Snakes coil in a jestful tease,
Bouncing bumps and playful knees.
They chuckle as the sun dips low,
Creating warmth in the evening glow.

With shadows high, the fun won't cease,
Dinner waits at laughter's feast.
A woodland gang, a merry crew,
In jolly twists, there's always new.

Follies of the Forest

In the forest, tales abound,
Where silly antics can be found.
A fox in socks, he struts with pride,
While a wise old owl, giggles inside.

Bouncing bunnies, cheeky and spry,
Hopping quickly, oh so sly!
They twirl around a mushroom ring,
Chasing laughter, what a fling!

A beaver with a bow tie bright,
Builds a dam with sheer delight.
As forest critters join the scene,
In playful chaos, all routine.

With every rustle, comes a cheer,
Follies dance when friends draw near.
In leafy realms where giggles grow,
Life's merry song, forever flows.

Parables of Play

In tangled vines, a story weaves,
Of merry hearts beneath the leaves.
A chipmunk tells a clumsy tale,
Of tripping feet on the winding trail.

A swing of branches, a jester's call,
Where nothing's serious, not at all.
With every hop and every skip,
The forest holds a playful grip.

A raccoon dons his mask with flair,
Stealing snacks without a care.
As laughter rings through every glade,
In this enchanted masquerade.

Through light and shadow, friends engage,
In parables of fun, they stage.
Nature's mime, a joyful play,
In teasing light, the world's at sway.

www.ingramcontent.com/pod-product-compliance
Lightning Source LLC
Chambersburg PA
CBHW072147200426
43209CB00051B/833